THE EBBING TIDE

THE EBBING TIDE

poems

CARLOS REYES

Cyberwit.net

HIG 45 Kaushambi Kunj, Kalindipuram

Allahabad – 211011 (U.P.) India

http://www.cyberwit.net

Tel: +(91) 9415091004

E-mail: info@cyberwit.net

Printed at Thomson Press India Limited.

for Bill Shenk & John Mercier

&

for Nancy & Helen in remembrance

Beginning With the Word *When*

When all the cormorants
have abandoned the fourteen
pilings they occupied and guarded
like sentries through rain, wind
and snow for the past two weeks,
does that portend something?

What happened while I slept?

When I said goodnight to Kincaid,
The Pyramids, Eureka and Lucky Chance
I wasn't praying to them — though I feel
they are oracles — but saying
goodnight to friends.

Eureka suggests I'll soon
make some earth-shaking discovery.

If I ever bet on a horse,
it'll be Lucky Chance.

When I got up this morning
the mountains were still there
reassuring me that some things
in this life we can depend on.

They give me hope that something
good will happen tomorrow.

This place is sound and sight:
herring season over, no noise of boats,
no jet plane leaving
vapor trails above the peaks.

The sky is only traversed by eagles
patrolling the Sound, the occasional
float plane passing.

These mountains watch over me
until the cormorants return
to keep their vigil over Thimbleberry Bay.

I might see snow melt,
but from this distance never hear
the rumble of avalanche.

From this cabin I can't see Polaris.
I'll take the snow-capped mountains,
almost as distant, untouchable as stars.

On an Island, Again

Baranof Island
in Southeast Alaska

in an archipelago
where the islands

look like shards
of ice broken,

suddenly shattered,
dangerous

jagged pieces
of translucent glass.

Rough daggers,
chipped obsidian

like all islands pointing

at my heart.

Shaped like a heart

a frozen heart

I could break with a stone.

Mt Edgecombe

It squats out there like Fuji
draping its ermine cape
that touches the water's edge.

Every fool white man
tries to possess it, to take it
from the Kiksadi Tlingit.

Spaniards, Russians,
British, now us,
try to name it, claim it.

In dim times the Tlingit
called it *L'ux* which
sounds like light, which

is what it is, or
flashing light, though
it went out centuries ago.

It is sacred to the Tlingit but
they know it belongs
to no one, it belongs to us all.

By one of the fourteen pilings
a small red boat, open
and left behind by the cormorants.

All is calm, perfect for a still life:
silver water, snow-capped green
mountains, wistful clouds, even better

under the full moon — clichéd yes, but still
with the incoming tide, the sliding boat
streaks for the shore but can't quite make it.

Then it slips back, pulled
by ebbing waters, while a fickle breeze
urges it away from the tide.

Our painting does not reveal the pencil
line that holds the boat to a piling: we
keep for a moment the illusion

of freedom. We hope that with the falling tide
some sliver of wind comes unbidden
from nowhere, will help it slip its moorings.

Teakettle, Whistling

White sailboat anchored out
front for two days shows no sign of life.

The teakettle whistling calls me away
from my lookout. When I return

the sailboat is gone. The whistle
a farewell to boats leaving or

a warning that another vessel is coming in.
The teakettle calls up days at sea

on the *Makin*. Skipper Sullivan said, *Boiled
is boiled, make your tea and shut off that whistling.*

Bad omen, a teakettle whistling
in a cabin empty but for me pacing the deck

before a window, glassing boats that anchor briefly,
sail on to other lives.

What Travels With a Woven Basket

In the carving shed
artisans collect strips
of bark they husk
from the cedar log,
put them aside.

As the log assumes
its other life as a totem, so
its bark takes on another
life as a basket, where essence
and spirit transfer from fiber
through skin, where oil travels
from deft fingers into fiber.

When the finished basket is taken
into a stranger's home, it
carries the diminishing
cedar scent and breath
of the person who wove it.

Remnant From the Carving Shed

I carry in my pocket
this chip of cedar
to anoint my hand,
for luck, a memory.

A guilty pleasure, this prize
secreted away. I didn't ask
if I could take it from the layer
of chips that soften our tread.

Like the rest, it has the imprint
of the carver's tracks and ours
as we walk in awe around
the evolving totem in the carving shed.

Gouged away in the shaping
of a straight red cedar log
into a thirty-five-foot totem,
this soulful fragment
I take with me when I leave.

It carries the carver's footprint,
the cedar's breath that fades
like sea fog burnt off in morning sun.

Headdress

And what am I to make of this tiara
of pure white, feathers spread like a hand

of open fingers? Nothing as elegant as the fan
of a bald eagle but carefully arranged

like a deck of cards, a hand of queens
on the muskeg at the base of a Sitka spruce.

The body long since taken, is
this then the spirit dampening beneath the tree?

It should be the other way around:
the body left, the spirit flown.

What am I to make of that? If it be
a tiara it's the diadem of the queen of hearts.

I'll steal one white feather for
a bookmark, a quill to pen another tale.

Morning unfolds in dramatic irony,
the players unaware of one another.

Out front in Thimbleberry Bay, a purse
seiner brings in his yellow nets of herring

roe to be shipped to the other side of the Pacific.

A Coast Guard helicopter practices rescue,
hopeful exercise, that man can rescue man;

lets a frogman into the water, winches him back,
though at one point he swings in an arc,

twirled in a carnival ride by blades
chopping the air into smoke-like vapor.

In front of both a humpback blows,
breaches, disappears into 300 feet of water.

The helicopter hovering hides behind the life saving
exercise, the spray its rotors make.

Dragging its scow, a fishing boat slips out
of the channel, cowers behind Marshall Island.

The humpback is oblivious
as we seine its caves, stir the air above,
chop the surface to a froth and mist.

Whatever it's up to
as it makes its way through the channel,
as it cavorts and frolics, the mist it shoots
twenty feet in the air dissipates in seconds.

The water we roil in the depths of Sitka Sound,
the oil and blood we leave behind,
the herring roe we take away . . .

Our hope of survival may be
the humpback whale patrolling
its domain, our dead end.

"The Table Is Set"

So says my neighbor
as we look out on Sitka Sound:
long before the cannon is fired

starting the race from the docks
to the nearby fishing ground where seiners
with eyes grown big envision thousands of dollars

to be scooped up in a brief season,
before the spotter plane flies over, before
the first fisherman sets his purse seine,

before the first pull of fish is spilled
aboard we know the winner: the hump-
back whale is already at the table

partaking of a feast
of herring.

leaves behind thousands of herring eggs
on strips of seaweed along the rocky shore
to let the sun finish the hatching.

I walk along until I realize
I'm treading on future generations of herring.
Were I a Buddhist I would be horrified

but I'm only a thoughtless ex-fisherman
looking for a snack.
The table is set for me, my

neighbor says. I say,
someone has dumped a truck load
of caviar in my front yard.

I pick up a strip of seaweed, draw
it between my teeth, bite each tiny egg.
As I taste each salty morsel

I am not guilt ridden. My poaching
is minuscule compared
to the harvest of seine fishermen,

catching herring, stripping their eggs,
tossing the fish aside to rot, while
the world goes hungry.

Newsies

Every afternoon, the crowd of paper boys
heads together, punching each other's shoulders

comes down Sitka streets to hawk
The Sentinel to passersby, cars, shops.

In 1945 I did the same in another city
bought newspapers for 3 cents,

sold them for 5 on the corner of the square.
I fought for the corner, a spot gained

through struggle, diligence, and time. With it
came the rush hour dream: the motorist

rolls down his window, hands me a bill.
In a hurry to get home, says *Keep the change.*

We made up headlines, catastrophes: *Tornado
Strikes Tulsa! Hundreds Dead!*

anything to sell a paper. When
real headlines hit our world: *War Over!*

Enola Gay Drops Bomb on Hiroshima!
nothing we made up could rival that. We stood

speechless on the four corners of our world,
saw our papers shredded

into a tornado of celebration. Buried deep
in our pockets, the copper heads of presidents.

Taken together
the islands of
Chichagof
Admiralty
Baronof
make up
a fish hook
the Tlingit
use to catch
halibut

Boats towed here, run aground
on purpose along the timbered shore,
tucked away in the salal

at the head of Silver Bay.
Licenses expired, insurance lapsed,
names and numbers faded by sea salt,

rain, snow or sanded away
begging for anonymity.
Too old to work, to pay

moorage, no hope
of salvage. Brass cleats,
winches, hydraulics stripped

for their final voyage, rude
docking here. The once proud
vessels of Nootka cypress, naked,

missing running lights, slouch
ill at ease. Half buried,
they rest here without tombstones.

At first I thought mercury
drops of water from
the mossy cliff above
hitting the mirror, the

face of Silver Bay.
Careful watching
taught me those droplets
were not falling down

but salmon smolt leaping up
in shadow for some insect,
invisible in afternoon
light, dying into night.

On a hillside above Sawmill Creek in April
we watch patrolling bald eagles,
talk geology, economics, timber.

He shows me a cold-deck
of logs he cut down
on Prince of Wales Island,
talks of stripping the bark

of Alaskan red cedar; how the
process reveals the wood's
musculature. He has confidence
enough to take his wife and sons

out with him trolling for salmon,
long-lining halibut. A man
of windburned face, his
rolled-up sleeves reveal

determination, resilience,
sinewy strength of cedar bark.

Russians logged this slope,
the skirt of Mt. Verstovia, made charcoal

to heat their Samovars.
Later they handed over

their residue — vast domains
they didn't own — to Americans from the south.

Hiking the trail today
my boot kicks up a small square of charcoal.

It is minuscule as historical detritus.
Hemlock, spruce, and cedar

grown up around the pit, the muskeg
almost buries it as the Russians buried

their dead in the shipwreck cemetery, left
St. Michaels and a building or two. But here

in New Archangel there are no descendants.

These Traces

— *After Yang Wan-Li*

Up this trail to Mt. Verstovia in the snow
I follow footprints until they disappear.

I carry on leaving mine, wondering who
will next come up this arduous path to wisdom.

At the Head of Silver Bay

At low tide
on the kelp laden rock face
asteroids cling
with suction cups,
holding on, waiting
for whatever life comes next
in 6 hours.

Liquid oranges, reds, pinks, blues,
a bumpy color wheel:
pastels left to dry,

as though the ocean
has been turned topsy turvy
by an earthquake or tsunami.

A crazy world whose floor
is now a perpendicular stony wall
with its creatures struggling
to stay together on something solid.

On Another Island, Baranof

– for Nancy

She was long marked by water
twice nearly drowned.

In Kansas she fell through the ice
on the Smokey Hill. In a coastal Oregon
stream she went down into a deep hole
almost drowning me.

Now on this first time back
to Alaska since her death
I watch the clouds cross
The Pyramids, feel darkness
drop onto Thimbleberry Bay.

One hundred miles east
in this same archipelago
between Petersburg and Wrangell
she left her life in the water.

When the floatplane went down
in questionable flying weather,

she was still belted in,
her husband lost
beneath the surface
of Stikine Strait.

Her sons took her back to Oregon, far
from Alaska, to bury her
beneath rain-soaked grass.

An Unexpected Visit

— On the first week in April the rufous hummingbird

visits Thimbleberry Bay

Helen finally tracks me down
on the same ocean but far north. She comes
visiting on a day of first sun, then rain, then sun.

She's been here before, though east in Wrangell.

All day she's tried to catch my attention as
I sneak into the dining room and watch.

I'm sure it's her but I don't want to startle her.

She's come a thousand miles on tiny, rapid wings.

How fast her heart is beating and mine too.
Now at last I recognize her, she is glad to see me.

How much better for her, this new life. Her other
one was often not happy but
she never lost her spirit.

As her daughter was seeding her ashes
into an icy coastal stream, she showed
once again her will, refused that river,
flew away with the west wind.

Fast beating heart, winged sister, Welcome!
I've put out honey for you.

This time I'll try not to frighten you.

If it rains, then clears
I'll look for you at the window.

Ketchikan Days, Nights

Two nights in the bars of Ketchikan —
time to sleep it off at the Gilmore Hotel.

Time to dance with women of sandpaper
hands, who work in the cannery.

Time to have a few in the notorious Fo'c's'le,
risk a fight, chance getting thrown in the pokey.

Time to walk the bridge over Ketchikan Creek.
If you catch high tide you can watch salmon

by the hundreds fight their way upstream,
all those fish heading home. But

if upstream is home, it's the funeral home.
Birth, death — food for the progeny.

Time to stand there and think
about the cycle. *Time*

to hear the flowing water when
it asks you the hard questions

about who you are and what
you're doing here

as the sun sets into the clouds
like oily change

on the dirty bar
in The Fo'c's'le.

In the dark I look across the water
of the Eastern Channel to the southeast.
Snow-capped Eureka Mountain at 9 p.m.
still shines against the gun metal sky.

The moon will forgive me this one time
if I say, as she rises over the waters, that her beauty
is no greater than the beauty of these mountains.

Such beauty: untouchable, inaccessible.
Right now you could never swim
the frigid waters, walk the snow drifts,
no way to get there from here.

Fourteen miles of Sitka Highway
runs from Old Sitka, a ghost town,
to the mill site at the mouth of Sawmill Creek,
not across the water to the mountains.

Beauty undisturbed, no one lives
on that mountain. What looks like
smoke from a cabin, a cloud tail. No ski lodge,
no strings of Christmas lights on the slopes,

no twinkle of passing planes, no fade of vapor
trails criss-crossing darkening sky, no white
patches of bandages scattered across the face
of a cut and bruised landscape, not here.

In the sky over timbered slopes, on the silver
surface above the caverns of the humpbacks,
tonight, as far as the eye can see: wilderness.

At this moment, nothing
like Baranof Island exists anywhere,
this shard of the continent,
accessible only by plane or boat.

Deep fiords abandoned by fishing boats.
Slopes of spruce and cedar. The snow
fields. At this moment, there is no peace
like it on the planet.

Early Morning Flight to Bethel

Among the few people
on the plane
are two girls
descending
from the darkness.

They speak Yupik:
you think
they are two moons
conversing.

You don't believe
in two moons for the earth
but you are half
asleep.

Perhaps it is the sun
speaking to her brother
who has lost his fire.

It is two sisters
speaking of a cruel winter

of eating muskrat
and cracking bones
of cranes, of hunger.

You see below
the wafer thin tapeworm
frozen to the brown belly
of the tundra.

They tell you
it is the Kuskokwim River.

To my untrained ear
the Yupik word *Kalskag*
sounds like gurgling, like the river.

But elbow of the river
is what it means, here
where they laid out the village.

When we return from a day
in the muskeg to a log cabin
built by Russian priests

we find a silver salmon
ready for the pan, a gift.

It is 11 p.m., the sun
just sunk into the Bering Sea.

Out on the Kuskokwim
the blue and white tug
The Tanana Chief rests

on its journey upriver
past Crow Village to Aniak, anchor
light bright as the pole star,
a constant for the Yupik.

The Chief's light on the river
our last slight connection
to whatever we left behind.

Sprites Visit at Noon

In from the bush we come in
for a bite of lunch.
Staying out is better — a chunk of
smoked salmon, rose hips,
high bush cranberries — but
we want something warm to eat
and a place to dry out.

The range won't light.

I try again and again, go outside
to the fifty-gallon drum, find
the butterfly valve is turned off.

Behind a beached fishing boat
beyond my peripheral vision:
Three sets of eyes, three
wide grins and giggling.

As I spin toward them
they flee like ravens clever,
like mosquitos and no-see-ums,
little sprites everywhere.

Déjà Vu, But Not Quite

Not far from the Bering Sea, far
away from Ireland, bog cotton
sways in the Southwest wind.

Inside this Yupik cabin
in a dark corner, the eternal
light, the glowing heart of Jesus,
JFK's face wreathed
in red plastic poppies.

It is so like Ireland,
so like Mary Lafferty
with her holy water
from our Lady of Lourdes.

George Urovak's
seventy-five-year-old mother
smiles, reveals
front teeth worn smooth
to the gums from a lifetime of
chewing hides for clothing.

She walks to me from out of the gloom,
holds a fist-sized grass basket,
offers me the gift
that took her six weeks to make.

Yupik Shadows

Some days in Alaska
there are no shadows.

That is why
in winter the Yupik quietly

walk through their villages
lanterns held high

calling *chamai, chamai.*
The white man thinks

it is only wind
through the snow drifts.

It is the Yupik trying
to convince the shadows

to return.

I.
Trying to convince mapmakers
to visualize what it's really like

on the ground; to prove
to them, that yes

in the boggy arboreal forest
small streams suddenly

spring up in the spongey surface,
just as suddenly disappear.

They question my notes:
What happened to that gurgling

short thread of a stream?
People who draw maps

don't like uncertainty.
It lacks closure, doesn't look

good on a contour map.
It is a question mark

without the dot.

II.
They get that puzzled look
when I can't tell them

to their satisfaction
where the ground is, when I say,

You have three choices:
the shifting mattress of the surface,

the slushy sand beneath, or the perma-
frost, solid ice, three feet down.

III.
The Yupik have the answer,
the last laugh.

George Urovak asks what we're doing.
Trying to find the ground, I reply.

He laughs, *It's what you're standing on.*
We know where we are. After sundown,

he says, *Look up,*
see the bright star,

the handles of the sled?
When we go outside at night

the sled is always there,
it's thrown over

so the dogs can't drag it away
while we sleep.

Where the Ground Is

Mapping the muskeg
up around Kalskag
on the Kuskokwim,

we tap the surface
with a leveling rod
to find ground.

I stand on a spongey
rocking surface until
I begin to sink.

At three feet down
we are still in peat
pushing with an iron rod

when we hit frozen earth,
the ground that never thaws.
We drive the rod

down so someone
can say *This is where it is,*
this is mine.

The Yupik laugh at this,
as if by driving an iron in the ground
you can own a piece of earth.

Might as well
try to buy
the North Star.

I'm unable to pronounce his name.
I have no Russian or Yupik to help me.
He has no problem with mine,
he says Carlos, laughs whole heartedly.

Today he makes Ptarmigan stew
the Yupik way. Simple:
pluck the bird, chop it
into pieces, and throw them all

into a black pot of boiling water,
throw in a handful
of salt and pepper, dust it
with spices as exotic as his name.

The large bowl of stew
is full to overflowing. Eating it
I separate the meat
from the bones with my tongue

and teeth, a treasure hunt.
Soon the bones heap up

taller than the bowl. He
picks through the pile

searching for a fishhook or
hollow wing bone for a whistle
then one by one tosses
the remaining bones

back into the pot.

April Days in Sitka

Single sentry, a bald eagle
atop a fuel tank at the airport
welcomed me earlier in April.

I've stopped counting the eagles
that come to watch over me.
Day and night I am attended

by black funereal bowed heads
of cormorants, overwhelmed
by the insistent presence of

hummingbirds that mark out
the hours each day for me,
goldeneyes that patrol the

dark water between the 14 pilings
looking out for me. But
this morning I am startled by

a golden crowned kinglet
perched outside my window.
Despite its royal sounding name

its crown is not gold. It's
a small modest bird, unusual
among the exotic ones here.

Honored to spend time
in the domain of the little king,
I bow, accept his appearance,

know he honors me
on my last days here with
an elegant farewell.

ACKNOWLEDGMENTS

"Carbon Footprint," On an Island, Again," and "Ketchikan Nights" first appeared in *Sea Smoke to Ashes* (2020).

"Yupik Shadows" was included in *The Book of Shadows* (2009).

"Early Morning Flight to Bethel" was first published in a slightly different form in *A Suitcase Full of Crows* (1990).

Abundant thanks to the Island Institute in Sitka, Alaska for the month-long writing residency awarded me in 2011. Many of these poems were written during that time and were published in *Connotations*, the Institute's journal. I am also grateful to Carolyn and Dorik Servid for their welcoming kindness and generosity.